This Handwriting Notebook Belongs To:

A

A is For

B

B is For

B is For

C is For

D is For

E is For

E is For

F is For

G is For

H

H is For

I

I is For

J

J is For

K is For

K is For

L is For

L is For

M is For

M is For

N is For

O is For

P

P is For

P is For

Q is For

R

R is For

s

S is For

T is For

U is For

V is For

W

W is For

X is For

Y

Y is For

z

Z is For

www.ingramcontent.com/pod-product-compliance
Lightning Source LLC
LaVergne TN
LVHW060154080526
838202LV00052B/4152